ALSO BY STEPHEN MANOJ THOMPSON

Land Of Opportunity Forever

Coma Story

Big Muddy 555

Customer Royalty

The greatest thing since sliced bread

Stephen Manoj Thompson, Ph.D.

Creative Commons Attribution-ShareAlike licensed (CC 3.0) and Copy Right © 2015 by Stephen M. Thompson, Ph.D. All rights reserved.

Published in the U.S.A. by OpenBeast.com, St. Peters, Missouri 63376

The author or the publisher does not claim the contents as a valid conclusion nor would assume any kind of responsibility for errors, omissions or irrelevancies. The advice and strategies contained herein may not be suitable for every situation, so consult with a professional where appropriate. Neither the publisher nor the author shall be liable for any loss of profit or any other commercial damage, including but not limited to special, incidental, consequential, or other damages. Furthermore the author had made every effort to contact authors/copyright holders of works reprinted or viewpoints cast-off in this book. This is not been possible in every case however and we would welcome correspondence from those individuals/agents whom we have been unable to trace.

ISBN-13: 978-1460934050
ISBN-10: 1460934059
Library of Congress Control Number:

PRINTED IN THE UNITED STATES OF AMERICA
1st printing: October 2014
10 9 8 7 6 5 4 3 2 1

Keywords:

Customer Service, Employee retention, Business case study, Loyalty marketing, Consumer behavior, Panera Bread Co.

Fine Points

Customer Royalty: The greatest thing since sliced bread is an "outside-in" observation on Customer Service. It's about proactive customer culture at Panera Bread® Company. The book's content or alleged comments are not endorsed by Panera Bread Company and/or its subsidiaries. All trademarks (including registered and common law marks) and special properties discussed/referred are owned by their respective organizations.

Contents

Foreword

Preface

Introduction

1	First things first	**27**
2	Bread winners	**47**
3	A friend in need	**69**
4	Technology at work	**85**
5	Bread as a gift	**101**
6	One Loaf at a Time	**117**

Foreword

The title of this book, Customer Royalty, not only defines the content of the contemporary business need, but it is also an explanation of customer importance in general. When Stephen Thompson told me that he was going to write a book on business, with a focus on customer service, I encouraged him without ado. He is a fantastic writer with a great eye towards detail. I always marveled about Thompson's tenacity and upbeat approach and this book is just that. He has presented a reasonable and practical customer approach for business effectiveness.

To the casual reader, this book will be impressive because of its common sense and simple attitude, but business practitioners will be astonished by the book's depth of detail and balanced complexity. Customer Royalty is a remarkable book; it is a business study and entertainment rolled into one.

Customer service is an important element for any organization. Many companies pride themselves on good customer service, but do little to systematize it and really turn it into something special. This book challenges businesses to think proactively and initiate every activity customer-focused as possible.

Customer Royalty is an inspirational read for winning customer loyalty, by encouraging a recalibration of business practices. It is an informative read for anyone starting a new company as well for seasoned business leaders. I'm excited about this book. Both it, and its author, will continue to be well-respected and well-used (the book I mean) resources in the years to come.

Kamal "Doc" Yadav, Ph.D.
Founder and CEO
Chemco Industries, Inc.
St. Louis, MO
Author: The Formula for Financial Freedom

"If you are living in a civilized world, then don't lose sleep over customer service"

- Stephen M. Thompson, Ph.D.

Preface

Known is a drop, unknown is an Ocean - Tamil proverb

Why one more book about CUSTOMER SERVICE or BUSINESS LEADERSHIP, when there are tons of outstanding books flooding the shelves of libraries and bookstores? Also be sure, not to forget e-books. Then again, why the same old style i.e., looking through a well-known-winning organization?

In this fast and chaotic planet, we formulate everything to sound more complicated, thus there is less room for rational and simple truths. In any case, it helps if certain basics are told repeatedly. This book is not all about business success; it's more on star sustainability. Customer Royalty is a straightforward causal read about provision of service to customers with an emotional and logical charge. It is a story about the leadership excitement instituted by a special group of people, whose success stands as a beacon for others. It's essentially many notches ahead of customer-satisfaction-level or bringing-customer-back themes, as it's on providing proactive service by foreseeing customer needs. Given the new age of social media, it is also essential to understand and complement new thoughts to ensure a delightful customer experience in our service-focused economy.

I approached this project as an outsider by immersing myself into the subject's operations. Though the studied company is widely recognized for driving the nationwide trend for specialty breads, the topic called "Customer Services" is the same for any business or language, and so I believe Customer Royalty is a valuable read. Acting as a consumer and interacting with employees and suppliers, allowed me to paint an unbiased and wide-ranging picture. Of course, studying a business from the consumer perspective is delicious when the subject is a "warmth" bakery.

Stephen Manoj Thompson, Ph.D.
Author, Land Of Opportunity Forever and Coma Story

Introduction

"The only people hiring right now are Panera Bread and Mexican drug cartels." That was the Word of Wisdom by the late night talk show basha, Conan O'Brien, at Dartmouth College 2011 commencement speech, while receiving his Honorary Degree. I guess ignorance is bliss. Like Richard David Bach, a legendary American writer, once wrote, "What the caterpillar calls the end of the world, the master calls a butterfly."

Anyway, one fine Monday evening, on NBC Nightly News, Ron Mott had a report from Clayton, Missouri, about Panera Bread Co. It was on how and why "Panera's Chairman, Ron Shaich, turned the Clayton Panera Bread location into a nonprofit community restaurant, based on a pay-what-you-can experiment." Relaxing on my sofa, after a long day, I couldn't believe I was paying attention for over one long minute. I often pick up the remote and change channels frequently. Plus I was missing Katie Couric then on CBS

Evening News. But hearing Panera's philosophy that "Everyone deserves the chance to eat healthy food while being treated with dignity," I had to momentarily put behind my Obsessive Compulsive Disorder. What fascinated me was the way Panera, hailing itself as a social enterprise, found its insights in a situation most of others would avoid. That was precisely when the idea of writing a book about Panera Bread sparked my mind. I quickly realized that many independent studies supported and applaud Panera's leadership in healthy choices in food selection, dining atmosphere and overall customer satisfaction. So soon my thought evolved into a "Customer Leadership" story on Panera Bread Co., which I consider worthy to propagate.

If you aren't aware, bread is one of the oldest prepared foods. What's more, the Lord's Prayer is, "Give us this day our daily bread." Well, bread is not just a staple substance consumed to provide nutritional support for our body. This "eternal" feed is the ultimate delight for any appetite. And no one realized better than Panera Bread that well-made bread by the catering industry is the centerpiece of a great society. They in fact took the bread industry and their customers to an enjoyable peak, perhaps no one expected. It's an undeniable fact that today Panera, as a large national chain, does have tremendous influence on how and what we eat. However, by offering seasonal and healthier items, Panera truly shines with its baked goods and does it all much better than any of its competitors.

If you haven't come across America's favorite bakery-café in your neighborhood, that's likely to change soon. Panera Bread has been expanding rapidly since its founding in 1981 (at times opening one to two restaurants every week), giving consumers a taste of artisan breads. Now that's what I call a "bread-winner." By the way, it's worthy to mention, instead of the usual red ribbon, Panera's opening ceremonies feature cutting a long baguette of French bread.

Panera's history starts with Ron Shaich's fist small sandwich outlet in Boston, which dates back three decades. That bakery soon merged with Au Bon Pain, which at the time operated three locations around the same area. Au Bon Pain, Inc. expanded and went public in the early 1990s. Then came the purchase of St. Louis Bread Company, a 19-store chain in Missouri. In 1999, the company was renamed Panera Bread, and has since expanded as a phenomenal national wide restaurant chain. No one would have guessed that a small group of bakery-cafes in the St. Louis area would become the fastest growing food franchise. With its national headquarters located in a suburb of St. Louis, Missouri, Panera Bread has made its mission, "a loaf of bread in every arm," a reality. Today Panera Bread along with its other groups, Saint Louis Bread Co.® and Paradise Bakery & Cafe®, operates and franchises retail bakery-cafés in 45 states and in Ontario, Canada. There retail products include fresh baked goods, soups, salads, innovative sandwiches, custom roasted coffees, beverages and related complimentary products. Panera restaurants are principally located in suburban, strip mall, and regional mall locations. With their identity rooted in handcrafted, fresh-baked, artisan bread, Panera indeed provides great tasting and quality food. By the way, do you know Panera all set to remove artificial additives from its menu, including artificial colors, sweeteners, flavors and preservatives? By the way, it needs some guts to be a trendsetter in attempting to fix our broken food system. Kudos to Panera Bread Co. Talking about guts, Panera's move on adding kiosks to its restaurants and introducing "order by phone" service is awesome, as that would help customers customize their food and prevent order inaccuracies. Well for regulars out there, don't worry about "would-be former cashiers" as they will now carry food to your tables!

Panera recorded an annual revenue increase of over 4%, with a net profit rise in excess of 25%, even during the infamous season of global financial crisis. This sleeping giant has gained a clear dominance in its business segment and went on to earn the title, "America's most healthy fast casual restaurant." With over 1,800 locations, Panera Bread is also one of the leading and recognizable brands in the nation (like Coke, Google or IBM). With a status of best-performing major-restaurant stock, the success of St. Louis based Panera is felt at the financial district of New York City as well. And along the way Panera has led the evolution of what has become known as the "fast-casual restaurant" category. An interesting fact I read was that Panara does not record franchise-operated net bakery-cafe sales as revenues. However, they do use franchise-operated and net system-wide sales information internally in connection with store development decisions and budgeting. Regardless, every location features high quality, reasonably priced food in a warm, inviting, and comfortable environment. Not to forget the signature comfortable gathering areas, fire place, relaxing decor and internet access.

In order to attain a uniform success the company obviously implemented various strategies, like identifying the opportunities and threats, analyzing the target market, determining position in the market, deciding on a growth strategy and figuring out the marketing mix. Interestingly, there was no special initiative on customer service. And there is a reason why? At Panera customer service is the way of life. The company's mission is delivering a unique warmth experience to its guests and one can experience it consistently every time. That's why I frequently remark, "Panera Bread is indeed the greatest thing since sliced bread."

Their amazing success and traditional leadership sustainability, even during off-putting economies, is remarkable. Though Panera's story is a byproduct of the free-enterprise-system, it was one man's spirited dream and self-conviction on delivering true customer experience that really shaped this revolutionary business. As in any business journey, it wasn't easy for Panera as there were many obstacles to overcome. In any case, there was no magic formula to this glorious episode, as it's just a simple logic that worked i.e., passion for taking care of customers.

The gist of this bread baker's conquest story is not necessarily about substantial business success. It is actually based on authentic leadership - leadership that is committed to perfection and to the improvement of customer service process, no matter how large or fast the business grows. The synergy created as a result multiplied the impact and compounded to a five star outcome and a new level of customer loyalty. Then again one shouldn't forget the frontline employees whose consistent effort to provide the best customer service possible, each and every day, makes Panera's business philosophy seem like an easy goal. If you would have noticed, the company's employees are highly motivated in providing proactive customer service i.e., they usually recognize the need of their customers even before it's expressed. This aspect is discussed in detail later, but a quick example is their spirit to address regular patrons by name. A while back, I came across an inspiring news article about a Panera Bread restaurant, in Little Neck, honoring its deaf employee Darryl Jennings, as associate of the month, in recognition of his superior job performance. In a letter of congratulations Vice President of Operations Greg George said, "Your continued support of our mission to wow every guest, every time is what will continue to make you and our company successful now and in the future." No wonder, Panera Bread consistently scores the highest level of customer loyalty among quick-casual restaurants, according to many professional research firms. From Business Week's *Customer Service Champs* to Fortune magazine's *100 Fastest-Growing Companies* listings, Panera has secured a permanent spot.

I believe Panera is a special story that needs to be told as there are quite a few replicable factors and elegantly fashioned customer service principles. As mentioned earlier, my inspiration for writing on Customer Leadership crystallized after watching Panera test market an innovative non-profit pay-what-you-can format. The company's noble thought at its core clearly represents an effort by Panera to give back to its communities by externalizing its core competency (which in Panera's case is opening quality restaurants).

Given the national scale of its operation, Panera generously seized the opportunity to turn their core competency against a societal ill. They made a small difference toward addressing the cause of food insecurity by providing an opportunity to pay whatever the customer wants, which helps folks who are the lower economy side. There are a bunch such stores already across the US. Though such kinds of social enterprise operations are a growing trend these days, I couldn't stop admiring Panera's proactive leadership - both from a social needs and corporate business perspective. Perhaps this is what Suzie Boss, a prominent social observer and journalist from Portland, termed as "retailing with heart." But I like the cool term suggested by Time magazine, "Robin Hood restaurant."

This non-academic plane-ride book, by and large is hence based on a Panera experience study, which intends to unlock the practical-minded perspective of customer service and the leadership that builds a strategic value for a winning business. What I uncovered was that Panera's business status is more than bread leadership; it's a perfect customer experience. At Panera customer is the central of gravity and they lead the way and set direction. Certainly Panera is much more than the comfortable, customer-friendly atmosphere, their signature salad, sandwich and panini lines, even the free wireless Internet. Likewise, what you would realize is providing excellent customer service experience is not a lot of work. The only thing that disappointed me with the Panera experience was that they don't serve wine! And I prefer to stay away from their caloric bombshell, Turkey Artichoke Panini - 740 calories, 26 grams of fat and 2,200 milligrams of sodium.

Being in a civilized society, we are obviously not in any customer service crisis, but it's still time for a proactive customer leadership revolution - as loyalty rocks!

Chapter 1

First things first

"We must become the change we want to see in the world" - Mahatma Gandhi (1869-1948)

My very first job title was "Associate Customer Engineer" and I was like, WHAT?

At the start of my career, undergoing on-the-job training for Novell Netware products, I was expecting a cool title; say Network Administrator or Product Engineer. For me the "Customer Engineer" label made less sense then, like DJ, which I don't get it even today (well, I am trying hard here to offend my disc jockey friend at my neighborhood cocktail lounge).

Anyway, being a newbie at the corporate world, I quickly assumed that "this whole customer thing" is some kind of a marketing or business ploy. Though I had experience as a customer, I did not necessarily understand how important the need is for a good customer experience or even what constituted a "decent" customer service. Without realizing, many times I had been on the receiving end of lousy service. Well, that was then and today I have authored a book on that very same topic. But enough about me!

Recently there were reports floating around about frequent sightings of an allegedly unknown animal in Puerto Rico, Mexico and the U.S. It's called the Chupacabras, whose name comes from the animal's reported habit of drinking the blood of goats and chickens. This legendary cryptid's buzz got so much attention that it's now being seriously researched in few universities. Not to forget, the popularity of the Chupacabras has resulted in it being featured in science-fiction movies and gone viral on social media.

Good or bad, real or hoax, and whether you like it or not, news travels fast and certainly rumors travel faster. This circumstance can be related to "customer perception." In this age of social media, one small unpleasant customer incident can lead to a huge business misery. On the other hand, unlike Chupacabras, customer perception has got an emotional element embedded in it.

I am a huge buffalo wing fan and I was a faithful frequent visitor of a well known "casual dining restaurant and sports bar" franchise, near my ally community. Though they are very good in terms of taking care of customers, my fanfare ended abruptly. The reason for the unexpected zero-balance-emotional-bank-account was, during our last visit on a busy Saturday afternoon, we got a table that was watery, literally soaked in water. It was so wet that their laminated monthly sports calendar was stuck on to the table. Due to the nature's wonder called "evaporation" our table did dry out eventually, say after ten long minutes. That one ill experience was enough to lose a loyal patron, though I am more forgiving in nature (certainly I am not complaining about evaporation). At that point it doesn't matter if they have a television above the urinal or not. What I am trying to emphasize is that "Customer Servicer" is undeniably a tough business.

On the other hand, many studies reveal that a typical dissatisfied customer does not even bother to complain directly; instead they instinctively tend to share their unhappy experience to a bunch of other potential customers. No doubt superior customer service is one of the most difficult deliverables facing the business world today, although it is attainable. By being proactive and applying some sound customer service and leadership strategies, any organization can increase its holdings in today's business environment. It's not any secret that business establishments need satisfied customers in order to survive, and so it needs to organize itself according to customer needs. Only such a mindset can encourage lasting customer loyalty.

Soon after the Stone Age, traces of "trust-based loose trading" were supposedly recorded, during both Bronze and Iron ages. Since ancient trade originated in the migratory patterns of prehistoric nomadic people, who ranged over long distances across the continents of Africa, Asia, Australia, Europe, North America, and South America, service and humanity played an unrealized part. Far away from the cradle of civilization and in the technological, cultural and demographic evolutionary period, loyalty and service were the instinctive response to the essential human need for social bonding, ritual gifting, cultural and economic prosperity. Thus service simply evolved as a *way of life*. Yet in our age it seemed as if we had to reinvent the concept and values of customer service.

What really happened and why the missing link? Maybe we just took things for granted and overlooked simple truths. Or let's blame it all on the 1930s Great Depression. Whatever the case may be there is no more avoidance as today consumer characteristics such as Quality Improvement, Customer Service,

Convenience, Competitive Price, Value and Communication Opportunities have practically converged. Thus an unforgiving need to create a new level of customer loyalty evolved.

Only by listening to customers and actively providing required product or services one can gain or retain market share. That's the modern economics-of-commerce scenario. Innovations, strategies and cool-trends are always subjected to change, but the need for quality consumer satisfaction remains the same. In fact, many experts now claim that quality customer service is the single most important factor in ensuring business success, even when weighed against advertising or marketing. In a competitive field, if one business courts customers with service and the others don't, it's the customer-oriented company that sustains. Then again customers typically feed the positive word-of-mouth grapevine about the quality service company. We all would agree that businesses couldn't offer everything to every customer. But once a profitable customer segment is identified, firms should not shy away from providing the best possible customer experience. More importantly, building customer satisfaction will be a lot easier if a loyal workforce is formed. Loyalty base can't be bought. It can only be earned!

In the present age, customer service is the only entry point for a successful business. As individuals, all of us use services, like going to the movie, drawing money out of our bank account, etc. Businesses also use services such as transport, insurance, and financial services. Common sense suggests that if we want to keep a business running, which is based upon a continual stream of customers, then it would be extremely beneficial to deliver professional customer service. So what is modern Customer Service and how to achieve a lasting Customer Loyalty?

First things first, i.e., understanding the basics. The Bible has practical instruction on how to treat others, including his customers. Interestingly, the fundamental concept of customer service isn't new or any kind of rocket science. It's the simple things we do normally on our regular lives (or at least supposed to). To be precise, listening, understanding and delighting. Basically it's the ability of an organization or an individual to exceedingly and consistently meet their customer's wants and needs. To put it blunt, if your customer is not treated well, they will inevitably leave your business for the competition. We need to really cultivate the ability to understand customer's needs and develop a process, if not outstanding service is nothing but a dream. It is a known fact that customers can either make or break a business, no matter how big or small it is. Without maintaining a healthy customer base even black-magic will not work. This is why it (not the back magic) is important to pamper your customers and treat them right. It doesn't hurt to include customer service planning within the marketing element and be treated as an important strategic tool. By and large a business earns more from their loyal customers than from anyone else. Believe it or not, most customers prefer good service to lower prices.

A recent research by an independent agency revealed that fewer than one in five people's purchasing decisions are ultimately influenced by getting the lowest possible price available through discounts and sales. The study further discovered that over 80 per cent of shoppers are looking to add value for their money when buying products through greater levels of customer service. Companies that give added service benefits are likely to be winners. They will definitely have a competitive advantage over rivals. The great thing about quality service experience is it doesn't have to cost much if an organization is creative and sincere. It goes without saying that there is a definite correlation between customer service and customer loyalty. Please do remember though customers can make or break a business, providing a decent customer service is so much easier than it sounds.

In today's economy, traditional paths to business growth, such as depending only on product and service innovations, are no longer as reliable as they once were. Focusing on creating a long-term partnership with customers is the lone option. In any business, customer service seldom rests in the hand of one or a few individuals. Every member of the organization forms a vital link in the chain that bolsters the effort to ensure cordiality and outstanding positive customer perception. Obviously that perception is primarily influenced by the customer's expectations having been met. Exceptional customer experience is not something that can be achieved artificially; it must be a priority throughout the organization starting at the top. By putting employees on top of the pyramid, any organization can hold on to talent while strengthening relationships with customers. Customer service initiatives must be recognized, admired, rewarded and emulated. It can only be sustained by being ingrained in the fabric of the company and should not be handled as a formality. In order for a culture of customer service excellence to grow and thrive, management must have a burning desire for it to be that way and the energy to ensure that this desire spreads throughout the organization and remains there permanently. If we look at companies praised for their exceptional customer service, what we could find is that those companies create a culture that supports excellence in customer service. Like commitment to strong organizational mission, hiring exceptional staff with high standards, communicating expectations clearly, and constantly immersing the organization with these concepts. It's not just training employees in customer service skills. What they do is ensure that customer service is interwoven into everything the company does. Customer service excellence simply becomes the way of life.

In today's world, customer service is an integral part of every job and should not be seen as an extension. It's the relentless task of selling good feelings and solutions to problems. Typically the front-line employees, especially those who work directly with customers, are the ones responsible for creating value. Hence management team should be more creative in empowering "value zone" employees. The positive outcome of empowering members of the frontline staff to serve as brand ambassadors and even crisis communicators can be seen in many reputed organizations. It essentially means giving some authority to front line staff, or simply showing employees more trust. Putting employees first should not necessarily be considered as an indirect way of putting customers first (though both are interlinked it's also two equally distinct business criteria). The needs of employees on the front lines would be the primary focus of a shrewd management team. Many companies have demonstrated that paying attention to value-creating employees is the best way to build profitable and sustainable relationships with customers. The concept of asking employees what they need to be consistently productive seems to be a difficult task for many managers. Believe me, there is absolutely no customer service without employee involvement.

Time and again I have heard criticism that customer service planning is comparatively easy and it's only getting employees to buy into the strategy is difficult. I agree that customer service is a long-term, everyday commitment that both employees and management needs to believe in. Then again, it's not really difficult to transit employees into a customer-oriented culture, and I declare that with the following sarcastic conviction.

The Taiwan's Environmental Protection Administration recently announced that, following the success of some trials in 2009, it is looking to have pig breeders "toilet train" their porkers, in a measure to reduce the volume of waste water generated by that country's six million swine. Apparently in their earlier trial a Southern Tiawanese breeder was successful in getting some of his 10,000 pigs to become potty trained. So, why potty-trained pigs are important to this customer service discussion?

They're not really, but I have a quick relevant story to share. About three decades ago, there was a situation in which a famous restaurant in Seattle wanted to improve all aspects of its service. When it came time to set service standards, they thought of trying something new, and that was to let their employees set the standards in their own departments. Even though management was somewhat dubious, which isn't a surprise, they let it go ahead and the results were phenomenal. Not only did the employees set more stringent standards than management had planned, the employees followed up and reinforced the standards they had set for themselves and their departments. They wanted to prove to management that they were intelligent people who had good ideas.

Investments in acquiring and training employees will only pay off when loyalty is built into the company's fabric. Customer loyalty, an old business concept, is the fuel that drives financial success even in this web-empowered business age. Strong customer experience is a business essential. Loyalty is a state of mind that helps increase market share, increases continued patronage and referrals. Customer service as a philosophy should be practiced by everyone, regardless. This means doing the obvious by treating the customers fairly and being friendly, flexible, informative, and ready to solve even non-business problems. More importantly, demonstrating a cool reflex when things go really wrong. The foundation one needs is one of courtesy, caring, willingness to serve, and an attitude that lets customers know that they do matter. Yes, there are studies and technologies that can help you put it all into practice, but great customer service has its basis in good manners.

Excellent customer experience is the ability to constantly and consistently exceed customer's expectations. Any company can benefit from a pragmatic, ethical approach of strong customer service practices, thus the positive cycle spins forward. A company's most vital asset is its customers and so customer service is indeed a hallmark of great business leadership. It's actually like a brand that the customer perceives and remembers of the service they received. True service endures through the best times and the not so good ones and in some situations even bonds mutual interests into shared goals. It's time we build a "service sells" mentality. And certainly not the one where we have to push "1" for English and after we do, we talk to an American-sounding-sales-rep in New Delhi, whose fist language might be English. These days there are more talks and emphasis on Customer Relationship Management and Customer Intelligence. Analysts who study and write about all this have increasingly recognized the importance of managing the customer's experience. Then again it has been proved that a customer's perception of an organization or service is built as a result of their interaction across multiple-channels, not through one channel, and that a positive customer experience can result in increased share of wallet and repeat business. So one can offer countless promotions and slash prices like crazy to bring in new customers, but unless one can get some of those customers to come back, no business won't be profitable for long. Outstanding customer service is the lifeblood of any business as customers are the most vital assets. In short, decent customer service means a customer's journey that makes the customer feel happy and satisfied, with a sense of being respected and cared for according to his/her expectation. This starts from the very first contact and carries throughout the whole relationship. Customer service is the informal keystone of our modern civilization (I didn't mean pop-culture) and so it should be our way of life anyway.

There is always something special about taking service seriously. Exceptional service companies will be the ones that will continue to increase their market share, retain their best employees and win over the hearts of their customers. To put it straight, our modern business world needs a makeover. So what should be the forthright approach? Its simple, the employee is number one, not the customer. Because happy employees would naturally provide superior customer service, right? For many businesses such commonsense proposal could even mean big cultural change. But embracing this thought, no matter how much work it will take, will deliver a competitive edge unlike any other. Remember that if employees are taken care well, they will take care of the customers. Then again, a large part of customer service success is creating a seamless experience. So even if the employees care enough, what if their hands are tied? They can't help or be creative. Providing appropriate authority and encouragement to exercise the same adds an ultimate level of customer experience. With all of the advances in technology, doing a good job isn't really good enough to stand separate from the pack. The big prize will go to the one creating new frontiers.

And well talking about "frontiers", let me share my recent confusing experience with an "all-Airbus fleet, ultra low-cost US airline". That was my first time flying on the so-called "animal concept" airline and rightly so I was kind off nervous. Mine was "Sal the cougar" flight (the airline puts pictures of animals on the tails of its aircraft). Soon my nervousness boiled into disappointment, and yes the rumor was right, they do play games with baggage fee, by obsessively sticking to their unsound policies. They seem to have mastered the art of extra fees. Long story short, I did end up paying an extra thirty five dollar for a small carryon bag. I understand airlines need to make money, but the way "Sal the cougar" got me was unreasonable. Anyway, am still sticking with them and that's not because they have the best deals to Trenton, New Jersey, rather for a timely customer oriented act. My onward flight was delayed (due to crew), and so after a few days later, I did get a hefty Electronic Travel Certificate via a surprise email, with a built-in apology. The compensation was based on the extent of departure delay it seems. After all the whole experience wasn't that bad, I guess!

Chapter 2

Bread winners

"Every company's greatest assets are its customers, because without customers there is no company" - Erwin Frand

The main strength of Panera Bread Co., I noticed, is that they have mastered the art of "effective customer interaction." Not only is the staff personable (as each staff member's role is carefully orchestrated, from cashier to line prep to store manager), but also they craft out a full fresh meal within no time. Nevertheless, a confession first: Prior writing this book all that I knew about Panera was that their bagels were big enough to make for a filling meal. In fact, for a while I had been involuntarily avoiding Panera. It's like one of those things where you're not really sure why or when it happened, but you crinkle when someone mentions the name and you immediately repeat it back to the person speaking it but with a question mark at the end! That had been my relationship with Panera Bread Co. On the other hand, I should also clarify that I was never a fixture at any Panera location, even while researching for this book.

One would have to be living inside a cave to not notice the positive phrase, "A loaf of bread in every arm." It is not merely a trademark or slogan, for the best-run fast casual dining restaurant, it is indeed the second nature of Panera's business culture. Based on their mission statement, I initially thought that they might be narrowly focused on bread and bread alone, rather than any social philosophy, customer experience, or any type of overarching purpose. Their simple trademarked mission statement also displays Panera's humble bakery origins. Not to forget their impressive so-called "bread leadership goal", which reads, "With the single goal of making great bread broadly available to consumers across America, Panera Bread freshly bakes more bread each day than any bakery-cafe concept in the country."

The focus of Panera basically lies in the wants of the consumer, which is healthy food made in store. Moreover, unlike most fast food chains, Panera understands that low prices aren't always the best value. Within a brief period, Panera Bread Co. has accomplished a distinctive position in the restaurant industry. What surprised me was even today, to further continue its growth, the company relies on first-time customers and word of mouth (or at least that's my take away). With food spending around 10% of a typical family's disposable income, the proportion of food budgets spent at home has increased since the onset of the recession. As the global economy is slowly recovering, America's favorite specialty eatery, Panera is opening more stores. Matter of fact, Panera has thrived through the recession in the fast casual market (restaurant between fast food and casual dining). It seems as if Panera team has discovered how to prompt our body to release opioids; a pleasurable chemical that temporarily soothes the brain and keeps us visiting them often. Sure that could happen when we eat any delicious comfort food; however at Panera the very same magic happens through their dedicated customer service, which warms our heart every time. I think Panera's success is on recognizing that customers want value and by offering an experience that consumers are willing to pay for.

I was once told that the number one smell for inducing nostalgia about childhood is the scent of fresh bread. Enter a Panera restaurant and you would exactly feel that miraculous sense. As soon as you walk into a Panera, you will see a display of freshly baked bread surrounded by a warm, inviting atmosphere with sofas, wholesome food, and fresh coffee. It's easy to tell that Panera wants its customers to stay for a while as they offer comfortable chairs, calming music, free Wi-Fi, and even meeting rooms. In my opinion, Panera's business concept is closely aligned towards the professed differentiation strategy, i.e. being unique in ways that a range of consumers finds it truly appealing. At Panera the value is provided to customers through unique features and characteristics of their product rather than by the lowest price. No wonder I used to think Panera Bread is a little expensive and just a status symbol for bread lovers. At times even now, when I visit them for a quick lunch, the price I pay leaves me wonder if I shouldn't have waited for dinner. More so when I order one of their simple panini and pay over dollar six. On a related note, Frontega Chicken is my favorite; it has smoked, white meat chicken with red onion, mozzarella cheese, tomato, chopped basil and mayonnaise all served up on a Rosemary and Onion Focaccia bun. Off course, it's served hot and smells absolutely wonderful. Well I almost forgot, with chips. Not sure why, but I only indulge with Panera's chopped chicken cobb salad when am on lunch meetings. So back to the topic of differentiation strategy, the reality is consumers indeed get excited about a quick, high quality dining experience and thus Panera became a delicious story. Obviously, companies that follow a "to be different" policy need to focus on consistent product innovation, including focus on top customer service and product quality. And that's exactly Panera is all about. Then again, given the nature of the industry, Panera's business strategy is kind of broad scope because they are forced to appeal to an extensive section of the market. Yet, they don't focus on matching and beating their rivals. To give a perspective, examples of other well known companies pursuing differentiation strategy are: Dr. Pepper, Caterpillar, Rolex, Mercedes cars, Wells Fargo Bank and 3M Corporation. Then again Panera's hard earned success did not take away their focus from customer service. And that's because the passion of taking care of customers and employees is their core principle.

At Panera Bread Co. earning "satisfied" customers is not good enough and they don't miss a single opportunity to put customers first. The result is millions of smiling faces and loyal customers. Sure there cannot and will not be a consistent or perfect customer satisfaction experience for every patron who walks into Panera, especially for a chain with tons of locations. It's pretty much impossible. But the emphasis here is that Panera is truly committed in delivering exceptionally high standards every time, and watching its pace of growth, it appears that its efforts in the customer service arena have paid off. Panera essentially has created value among the customers by satisfying their literal needs and demands. That's why regardless of their uninterrupted successful ride they regularly change trends to excite customers, by giving new features. Like toned decors (not to forget the signature fireplace), comfortable couches, and also current newspapers. The thing that always strikes me, as I walk in, is that the restaurant is filled with natural light. I am a big fan of sunlight over fake light. It has a noticeable effect on how one feels. Secondly, the menu features a wide variety of made-to-order sandwiches prepared with freshly baked artisan breads, desserts, crisp salads, homemade soup and gourmet beverages. Thirdly, unlike other casual restaurants, food is served in baskets or in china plates and cups, and customers eat with silverware. Then comes my favorite, most Panera outlets offer Wi-Fi facility with their unpretentious atmosphere. At Panera there are no rush, and more hours means selling more coffee and cookies. I consider all these as customer centric approaches, which had helped its business grow and sustain. All these actions essentially prove that Panera is clearly in the business of building relationships and trust with customers. Well, we don't see that on their mission statement though.

With Panera's identity rooted in handcrafted, fresh-baked, artisan bread, they claim to be committed in providing great tasting, quality food that people can trust. That exactly why, nearly all of their bakery-cafes have a menu highlighted by antibiotic free chicken, whole grain bread, and select organic and all natural ingredients, with zero grams of artificial trans fat per serving, which provide flavorful, wholesome offerings. In addition one can trace the roots of most dishes on Panera's menu to its R&D team's twice-yearly retreats to the Adirondacks, where staffers take turns trying to one-up each other in the kitchen. Panera Bread was actually the first national restaurant concept to voluntarily put calories posted next to their items on menu boards nationwide. Apparently their focus is to be as straightforward as possible, so that customers can enjoy it even more. It's because of proactive customer centric efforts Panera frequently get recognized as a health-and-nutrition leader, as well as for being a place to get delicious food. What's more, Health magazine named Panera Bread Co. the number one healthiest spot for eating on the go.

Speaking bout nutrition, do you know every Panera associate would be able to articulate flawlessly and confidently about nutritional information of any Panera product? Sure they do have a novel online Nutrition Calculator as well. But the point to take note is the enthusiasm and preparation of frontline employees.

For organizations to develop they require a clear and supportive direction. The business leadership provides the direction by taking responsibility for making decisions and running a business well, which is certainly a momentous skill. What I observed was Panera places considerable emphasis on getting the right people with the right skills into key posts. To be more definitive, they kind of have built a sub-culture in which those who don't share their core values are literally surrounded by anti-bodies and ejected like viruses. I have also observed that they tend to hire people who are already predisposed to similar standards and keep them. They also ensure that these people have the opportunities to develop decision-making skills. Equally, this means that they take great care in saying what they will do, careful never to over commit or to promise what they cannot deliver. At Panera employee promotions are usually based on "total" customer satisfaction. Promotions and salary increases are, for the most part, directly tied to customer satisfaction ratings and store performance. It is so stringent that even if a store had great revenue but earned a low customer rating then no one from that branch gets a raise. By the way at Panera raises are offered every six months. The result, employee DNA's are permanently altered to be productively neurotic, self-motivated, self-disciplined and compulsively driven to excel. That's why you would usually see Panera people display remarkable intensity and create a positive cycle. Last winter when I was casually chatting with a Panera manager, at a relatively new location in St. Peters, Missouri, I noticed a peculiar confident attitude. He kept emphasizing the store's quick success to his hard working people. Almost for every question I put forth he pointed out, giving credit to factors other than himself; essentially shining a light on others who also contributed.

Promoting and offering career opportunities from within the company had a positive effect on Panera. That's also reflected on their jobs website, "Panera Bread is a specialty concept with unparalleled people and quality products offering careers as diverse as our breads." Time and again studies have shown that happy employees will stay longer and always give their best. With career path linked to customer satisfaction rating, employees give close attention to customer experience. Every new store associate goes through a mandatory paid employee training session before start work where they learn about the company and first day's job tasks. Of course they then get to sample lots of Panera food then. Actually every new store employee gets dough training. And meetings start with the staff breaking bread together. However my favorite is employees get a 65% discount on meals. Also the wage rate is claimed to be always higher than their closest competitor. Employees who put in at least 20 hours a week get health insurance, 401(k) savings plan, and discount if they buy company stock. Then again there are frequent training and mentoring sessions by local store managers. Not to forget, senior employees go through advanced training program that surprisingly teaches how to run their own business. It's very common that within few years many have risen to the top level of retail positions. This company is very good at promoting from within to strengthen the team. Furthermore, Panera makes every effort to ensure that its workforce is representative of the cultural and ethnic diversity in the wider population. That also helps to develop a "culturally aware" workforce. Panera managers are encouraged to look for employees showing signs of disengagement so they can take immediate action. It's very common at Panera a manager buying meal for an employee as a goodwill gesture. The leadership recognizes that motivation is personal to the individual and a motivated workforce does not just happen. People need to be encouraged. By actively listening to the employee's ideas, they may be able to make changes that will motivate the employee. Panera encourages managers to motivate their teams throughout the working day. They essentially created the right environment for motivating and engaging its people through the development of good communication channels, appropriate training and honest and timely feedback. It's not a coincidence that Panera Bread usually gets the #1 ranking on J.D. Power and Associates' Annual Restaurant Satisfaction Survey.

Besides, many such benefits help keep annual turnover substantially very less compared with the industry average of 190%. Panera Bread Retail Satisfaction Survey persistently shows that over 90% of their retail management associates are "highly satisfied" with their careers at Panera Bread Co. Thus amazing customer positively, and doing it with enthusiasm, has become a way of life inside Panera. Essentially a culture of commitment was formed.

The leadership at Panera had to do no acid test as they primitively grasped the cause-and-effect relationship between Customer and Employee Satisfaction at the very early stage. The impact of employee attitudes on the satisfaction levels of customers cannot be overstated. They realized that to achieve great customer service all that matters is satisfied employees. Then again it can only happen through volunteerism, as enthusiasm or devotion can't be forced. Panera needed to consider service as a practice and relationship building. That's exactly why they have a strong focus on opportunity for employee growth. The company's leadership spends considerable energy on empowering its employees and leading by example. Consequently Panera's comprehensive customer service program evolved, with the participation of its employees, which gave a timely competitive advantage. Thus its bedrock business values proved brilliant.

Panera believes that customer satisfaction is an investment, which is equivalent to research and development in manufacturing sectors. Customer experience is an important part of their culture and local community customers come back to Panera time after time. More than that, Panera's loyal regulars invest energy and commitment in recommending to their friends. There is no better way of promoting a business than through word-of-mouth recommendation. Panera is a big company that has the approach and feel of a small business. So each employee has an important role to play.

Creating and sustaining a service operation is a difficult task, as it is a performance that needs utmost passion, but Panera makes it look too easy. The pointer we need to take note is the method in which it's done, and that is the friendly attitude of its motivated employees. Motivated employees benefit the company in more that one way, i.e., working with passion, coming up with new innovative ideas and last but not least moving the company forward.

Getting back to the online Nutrition Calculator, which superficially makes Panera stand apart, was indeed an after effect of a frontline employee's suggestion. Panera was amount the first to do the online nutrition. They also have a formal program called "make it better" and all the employees can suggest an idea to make the restaurant better. Not to forget the professional appearance on their staff and khaki Panera cap. Interestingly, studies show professional look helps put customer at ease and demonstrates confidence. Though it's a very fast paced work environment, Panera employees in my observation, are somewhat casual (in a positive way) and are very friendly and that's their hidden strength I would guess. According to several independent studies, an overwhelming percentage of customer states that they are completely satisfied with Panera experience. To my surprise, it was not the free Wi-Fi or even the quality of food that drives Panera experience's statics high, rather it was the staff behavior that leads.

At Panera Bread Co., its fundamental values are taken very seriously in treating their employees. The leadership makes it a point to share "Panera warmth" by showing sincere care in everything related to their employees.
The associates at Panera are rewarded on the basis of giving customers what they want - outstanding service. With a mission to look after their customers and employees, a culture of outstanding customer service has been firmly adopted as a way of life. The company has been providing the industry-leading compensation and benefit programs for over two decades now. Panera to date continues focusing on two crucial ingredients, i.e., customer service and treating their employees

with respect and giving them opportunities to advance.

Many times one would notice excited Panera employees wandering through the café offering warm samples. That kind of a paraded passion has a trickle-down effect on Panera brand. Then again I noticed a motivating aspect that seemingly adds up to Panera's extraordinary high employee satisfaction. At the end of the day, the employees get to take home whatever baked goodies are left over, as well as my favorite paninis (both frontega chicken and the portabella mushroom). Whatever the employees don't take home gets donated. On a relate note, at Panera there are no preservatives in the baked goods, so they don't last long.

Fundamentally, Panera's leadership strongly believes their commitment in maintaining staffing levels and competitive compensation for their associates is the answer for current and future success. Management is about getting things done. Leadership is about achieving goals by creating a direction for a business and inspiring employees to take initiative and make the right decisions. Panera managers need the skills to motivate, lead and influence others. They also put a high value on teamwork and open communication between employees at all levels. Panera basically employs motivated individuals with the potential to become good leaders. That said the company provides its bakery-cafe operators the opportunity to share in the success. Through a cool Joint Venture Program, selected general managers and multi-unit managers are provided with a multiyear bonus program based upon a percentage of the cash flows of the bakery-café they operate. Thus far the company is convinced that the profit sharing program did create supplementary team stability, resulting in a higher level of consistency for respective bakery-cafe. Panera's management also feels that the program leads to stronger associate engagement and customer loyalty. Currently, approximately fifty percent of Panera-owned bakery-cafe operators participate in the Joint Venture Program.

Obviously this recipe is succeeding at Panera. That's why while its competitors are scaling back on upscale ingredients, trimming portion sizes, and creating value menus, Panera is selling fresh food and warm bread at full price. Today Panera Bread Co. has evolved as a community gathering space and as well as a bustling lunch spot. It's like they are renting space to people and the food is the price of admission with free outstanding customer service.

Lately, I came across a story of a Panera Bread restaurant at Little Neck honoring one of its employees, Darryl Jennings, as associate of the month, in recognition of his superior job performance. In appreciation for Jennings outstanding service, he received a certificate of distinction, a $50.00 cash prize and a gift certificate for two at a Panera restaurant. In a letter of congratulations, Vice President of Operations Greg George said, "Your continued support of our mission to wow every guest, every time is what will continue to make you and our company successful now and in the future." Now all this sounds usual. But what if I say Mr. Darryl Jennings is a deaf person? Yes, the honor was on the one-year anniversary of Jennings employment with Panera. He was introduced to Panera Bread by Lexington Center for the Deaf Vocational Services. Despite his sensory disability, he proved himself an excellent employee and team member. The gradual training he received with the presence of an on-site job coach (by Lexington) to facilitate communication allowed Jennings to learn, retain and perform his job duties in food preparation and kitchen maintenance with excellence, resulting in his recognition as associate of the month. Now isn't that something get excited for! I can keep going on with many such inspirational employee centric stories about Panera.

The again, no process can be one hundred percent perfect. And so is any customer service effort, no matter how hard an organization tries. A point of case, recently a man was accused of exposing himself to customers in Newport News Panera Bread.

Yes, I got a bunch of such stories as well. But what really shocked me, about this bizarre or rather eventful incident was, our hero (32-year-old, Derrick Lamont Parker) was accused to have done his humble act previously to few other Panera customers, over those past few weeks. The last I heard was he got released on bond from the Newport News City Jail. Just to clarify, Mr. Parker wasn't a Panera staff.

In any case, Mention Panera Bread Co. and fans are most likely to praise their customer friendly employees than their renowned free Wi-Fi or even the appealing Asiago cheese bagels; well I might have meant the hardcore fans. It's clear how Panera became the dominant player in the market today. Try adding up the sales for the next four biggest bakery-café chains and they'd still be less than half of Panera's sales. Panera knows how to take care of its breadwinners and thus emerged as a bread leader and financially been on a high roll.

Chapter 3

A friend in need

"I don't know what your destiny will be, but one thing I know; the only ones among you who will be really happy are those who will have sought and found how to serve" - Albert Schweitzer

A prominent business journal recently commented Panera Bread as the Apple of casual dining, and I tend to agree. Panera Bread's signature, i.e., specialty breads and affordable, gourmet food selections and awesome customer experiences puts them in a class its own. At all times Panera approaches its service differently so as to differentiate itself from competition. As mentioned earlier, one of their approaches to restaurant industry is the philosophy of placing customers and employees first, which they put a lot of effort into recruiting and training. On the whole their model is to hire motivated individuals and teach them to run a business by delivering exceptional customer service. With perfect customer satisfaction, customers will be sure to come back, and with employees who are happy, well-informed, and part of a team atmosphere, they will provide the best service possible. This phenomenon can be mischievously related to the suicide grasshoppers brainwashed by parasite worms' effect. French biologists have discovered that hairworms, which live inside grasshoppers, pump the insects with a cocktail of chemicals that makes them commit suicide by leaping into water. The parasites then swim away from their drowning hosts to continue their life cycle. Now sci-fi screenwriters may have a new role model or can replace the terrifying creature on the Alien movie.

The modern lifestyle choice to eat healthy has earned a natural positive impact for Panera

Brand. The company had also always focused on five key benefits for the customer:

1) Providing an affordable treat in a warm, inviting, and comfortable environment.

2) Giving customers a reason to return. Panera frequently introduces new products with fresh ingredients (I couldn't resist mentioning their lobster sandwich here).

3) The most beneficial attribute is the Wi-Fi internet access, which earns the bread cafe big bonus points.

4) Timely service, which is only possible with enough and motivated staff, by continued investment on labor and quality of people.

5) The convenience of many locations with a strategic emphasis on being a "neighborhood gathering place."

Certainly Panera's success can be attributed to its sensible evolution, but there is one extraordinary characteristic that seemingly got unnoticed, even by its competitors. Many times the real attributes of a company's culture and policies can be identified only during the time of need. The great known unknowns about Panera were revealed in recent years, and I would like to highlight a few.

With economic gloom descending and many outfits in the restaurant industry struggling, Panera fared better than other chains. Actually they added more stores to its growing network during the so-called modern recession, and stayed stronger. Now that's not a fairytale. But what if Panera comes up with a concept of "shared social responsibility" and opens up a couple more soup and sandwich restaurants with a pay-what-you-can format? That's exactly what Panera did by test marketing an innovative non-profit Panera Cares community café format in the midst of a struggling global economy. The company's noble thought at its core clearly represents an effort to give back to its communities by externalizing its core competency, which is opening quality restaurants. Given the national scale of its operation, Panera generously seized the opportunity to turn their core competency against a societal ill, so as to make a difference toward addressing the "cause" of food insecurity.

Panera Bread Foundation in now rolling on in top gear with it's newly formed Panera Cares™ community cafe initiative. What this inspirational initiative proves is that companies can and should do more than just donating or writing a check for social needs or disasters. In fact, this model would serve companies far better by leveraging their skills and expertise to make a more direct impact.

Don't be surprised if you find things are a little different during your next visit to Panera. Chances are you might see a menu board that no longer has prices but *suggested donations* and no cash registers, as that could be the café representing the social experiment executed by Panera Bread Foundation. At Panera Cares, customers are given a suggested donation amount for their order and can leave whatever they deem to be their fair share in one of the donation bins located throughout the cafe. According to Panera Cares it's not about offering a hand out rather about offering a hand up to those who need it. Panera calls them, "community cafés of shared responsibility". These cafés look like any other

Panera restaurant, with same menu, same customer friendly associates and comfortable environment. Their community restaurants utilize Panera's distribution system, thus access to its national food suppliers. Panera Bread Foundation is determined to open a similar location in every community it operates. With this innovative switch from the for-profit Panera Bread operation to a non-profit Panera Cares, all profits are being donated to local charities, and down-on-their-luck people can eat for little or no cost.

Technically Panera Foundation pays the new restaurant's bills, including staff salaries, rent and food costs. At the end of each month, the foundation tallies donations to see if they cover food costs. To date, these catalyst cafés are working as intended. Essentially neighbors are taking care of one another, and these cafés are proving sustainable as a catalyst. As it read's in their web site, "Panera Cares exist to make a difference by offering the Panera Bread experience with dignity to all - those who can afford it, those who need a hand up and everyone in between". Isn't that something?

When companies walk the walk of corporate social responsibility, in the long-term such efforts will increase business value and so it can be cynically termed even as an enlightened self-interest. The timely initiative of Panera Cares is one that symbolizes a positive movement of great importance to society. With such inspirational leadership goodwill efforts like Panera Cares, the trend is sure to become a norm for the corporate world. In point of fact, one would be surprised to realize that at the first Panera Cares Café near St. Louis, it seems about 20% of customers leave more than the suggested donation, about 60% leave what's suggested and about only 20% leave less. In any case such not-for-profit humanitarian cafe is a great idea especially during difficult economic times and periods of high unemployment and need. But what impressed me was the truth sprouted about humankind due to this business concept, i.e., people can be decent. Panera Bread has set a commendable example for others. No doubt, feeding hungry people for free is about the best publicity a restaurant can get. However, the selling point to adopt this concept was not about getting good press, but about doing right by the people in the communities in which a business operates. Imagine if more and more business corporations get active in trying to address social needs, like the Panera Cares model. Off-course, such fundamental-goodness-of-people-effort comes with a huge risk. Panera's noble experiment in pay-what-you-want retail has been successful at its first two restaurants in St. Louis and Detroit. However, the third free-will restaurant in Portland, Oregon was not attracting enough paying customers. In any case there are a few followers already, like Jon Bon Jovi's Soul Kitchen in New Jersey.

Panera shows its appreciation for customers not only within their bakery-cafes but also throughout the communities they serve, and Panera Cares is just one thriving charitable offering out of many. At Panera Bread, giving back to local communities is a creed. Their in-house philanthropy, Operation Dough-Nation was founded in 1992 to formalize their scattered and non-formal community involvement activities. Since then, it has progressed into formal programs such as Community Breadbox™ cash collection boxes, the Day-End Dough-Nation™ program, gift card fundraising and regular community events. Actually Panera's marketing goes against traditional brand-building, with giving back to the community, through Operation Dough-Nation playing a major part.

The Community Breadbox program ensures that donations made at Panera Bread feeds back into the community. A portion of cash donations made by customers in bakery-cafes gets matched by Panera and distributed to local non-profit organizations. Within the initial few years Panera was able to donate more than a million dollars, with contributions generated through this fitting program, providing basic necessities for those in need. Each bakery-cafe has a Community Breadbox collection container at each set of registers, encouraging customers to donate to a critical non-profit organization in the community. It turns out that today one of the major activities of Panera's community outreach effort is the Community Breadbox cash collection boxes.

Day-End Dough-Nation program is my personal favorite though as it combines corporate giving into product-centered community involvement. Giving back thus happens on a daily basis at Panera Bread as at the end of every day, the bakery donates high-quality, unsold bakery products, which are packaged to food banks and other non-profit, tax-exempt organizations that help people in need. In recent years the restaurant's collective annual donation adds up to a retail value of over fifty million dollars worth of bread and baked goods to charitable organizations, helping to address the need for food distribution in local communities. In fact, many outside individuals and community groups work with Panera to help deliver on a weekly basis. This end-of-day donation practice means this company uniformly give back to each and every respective community in which it operates.

I am starting to feel that it is my duty now, to support companies that give back so much to their local communities. It is a good thing for me to give in to my cravings for Panera's orange scones! In any case Panera's posh trade mark of Universal Spirit of Bread is Sharing® is difficult to practice, yet well demonstrated.

SCRIP fundraising is one more proud participation of Panera, helping non-profit organizations raise money. On the whole, this popular fundraising program invites non-profit organizations to pre-purchase Panera Card® gift cards at a discounted rate and then re-sell the same at full price.

In addition Panera leadership regularly makes the conscious and accustomed in-kind donations to local community events, such as silent auctions, runs and walks, trivia nights and raffles. From my outside-in observation, it looks like the normal corporate citizenship practice gets more visibility than Panera's innovative programs. Nonetheless there is a special touch in whatever Panera does, as not all charity or customer-centric initiatives are instigated by its corporate leaders. In fact many corporate approved programs were set off by its motivated and empowered store managers or franchise owners.

That said I would like to highlight Panera's famous Pink Ribbon Bagel®. We all know that the pink ribbon is an international symbol of breast cancer awareness, but what is this odd-sounding pink bagel?

The creation of the pink bagel came about from a casual fund-raising brainstorming discussion by a franchise co-owner, who is a cancer survivor. With the help of her local store bakers, the idea developed into a recipe; cherry chips, dried cherries and cranberries, honey, brown sugar with a subtle vanilla flavor. That first year alone, over twenty-five thousand pink bagels were sold. Not only did they win the, "You Can Make a Difference Award," from Susan G. Komen for the Cure, the well-known breast cancer association, but Panera Bread adopted it corporately in 2005, refining the recipe and shaping it into an actual ribbon. What's more, in 2009, Panera Bread bakery-cafes collectively sold over 1.3 million of those bagels, during the National Breast Cancer Awareness Month. In Panera's language, "It's sweet in every way". Recently they celebrated ten years of fighting breast cancer by baking bagels. Which accounts for more than 7 million Pink Ribbon Bagels; $1 million raised since 2001. These bagels feature cherry chips, dried cherries and cranberries, vanilla, honey, and brown sugar, and are baked fresh early each morning.

Panera Bread indeed strives to support community programs that reflect their core values and serve as a vehicle for outreach and support. The culture that led Panera evolved in this fashion, in fact, strengthened the customer bond that kept it intact and vibrant even in difficult economic times. If noticed carefully, in every community or customer centric situation Panera employees have an unspoken backing from their leadership for doing the right thing. When employees are empowered to make decisions, it improves their sense of worth and self esteem. It also helps them to use creative skills within their role and motivates them to perform better. Making decisions at a local level helps to meet customers' needs and enables individuals to take a pride in their job. Unlike the autocratic style of leadership, where a manager makes a decision alone. Otherwise how can an ad-hoc wedding happen at a Panera restaurant? Yes, that's right a couple from Florida had their wedding ceremony at a Panera in Orlando.

Actually the wedding was planned in an outdoor ceremony at Lake Eola in Orlando, Florida, but Mother Nature had a different say. Tropical storm Fay arrived precisely at the wrong time, with a clap of thunder, the skies opened up into a torrential downpour. Totally soaked, the guests were forced to run for shelter all round. The shocked couple-to-wed seemed to roll with punches. And yes, there was a warm, classy, nice and dry Panera nearby, with welcoming arms. Realizing the plight of the wedding party, the manager was willing to let them get married right then and there. As quick as a cheetah, the manager jumped into action and invited the entire wedding party to come in the restaurant. Her employees brought out dry towels to help the wedding guests clean up and dry off. Luckily (to use the word loosely) because of the rain the store was not that crowded. So that made it a bit easy on rearranging some tables and creating an aisle with white runner through the back swiftly. The Unity Candle was set up on a trash can, which Panera folks quickly decorated. They turned up the classical music and the patrons of the restaurant, the employees, and the guests stood, applauded, and celebrated, as the thankful couple took their vows. After the ceremony the manager offered free coffee and cookies for kid guests. Though it sounds to be one of the most unusual weddings, it is not an entirely unusual authorized act exhibited by those Panera employees. Stepping out of their everyday role, and making an unplanned wedding a reality, was just a natural instinct to serve above and beyond. I am sure the wedded couple would thank Panera, every time they look at their wedding pictures. Besides, now I am convinced Panera can be called a "Fast-Casual Family Restaurant" as well.

In passing, rain on a wedding day is a superstition said to bring good luck; cleansing or stronger unity in the marriage and it foretells the coming of children just as rain promotes growth in the farmer's fields.

Chapter 4

Technology at work

"Do what you do so well that they will want to see it again and bring their friends" - Walt Disney

The restaurant business is a competitive industry. Literally hundreds of restaurants compete with Panera on a national, regional, and local level. To stay profitable, Panera regularly reviews and revises its menu and subsequently responds to customer needs. To stay unique, the company developed an atmosphere that would encourage people to hold meetings or do work at the restaurant. Since buyer's bargaining power is relatively high for Panera, the restaurant constantly stays in tune with customer preferences and with control. On the other hand, Panera's suppliers have a relatively low bargaining power because Panera implements a lot of controls. Panera controls the quality of their main product by making the bread themselves daily. Also, the company contracts with numerous suppliers to keep an individual supplier's bargaining power low. In addition to the dine-in and take-out business, Panera offer Via Panera, a nation-wide catering service that provides breakfast assortments, sandwiches, salads or soups. Via Panera is supported by a national sales infrastructure with an assured growth prospects.

Recently there has been a collective push for healthier eating in our society and Panera adapted to that trend proactively. A wide variety of salads, healthier meats and better bread options was its opportune answer. Additionally, Panera's high brand quality makes it unconsciously easy for customers to recognize healthier options thanks to the tons of (sometimes presumed) unhealthy fast food chains.

Customers in general tend to patronize those businesses with a reputation for meeting or exceeding expectations. Plus, excited customers are an excellent source of referrals. Customer loyalty drives business, and technology is indeed an important component on how that is achieved. In earlier days, when customers wanted to contact a company, they would simply pick up the phone, dial an 1800 number and be promptly directed to the "next available representative". Now that reminds me of two things; the NBC sitcom "Outsourced", and the modern business trend of outsourcing "hello girls" jobs (call centers, I mean). Sure, many big companies reportedly save a bunch of money and everybody is happy - except their customers! Anyway, let me not get into the "outsourcing anxiety", which has become the fact of our modern life.

Today's customers are more informed than ever, and the rising popularity of social media is radically changing the way customers interact. Wireless public Internet service started popping up, only a few years ago, becoming a mainstay of the posh coffeehouse or corner café. However, one would be surprised to realize that Panera Bread Co. was not an early adopter of Wi-Fi. Getting new ideas implemented, even when it has obvious advantages, is typically difficult. Technology innovations especially require a lengthy period, often of many years from the time they become available to the time they are widely adopted. Like many companies, Panera had focused on internal processes, such as accounts receivable and cash receipts, when it first started its automation efforts. Years later, Panera's leadership committed to molding the company's systems to support customer satisfaction. As executives were grappling with whether or not to expand its Information Technology investment, a frontline manager's suggestion suddenly put everything in perspective. The manager observed that the customers would spend more time if internet access was provided, thereby filling in the chill-out time between breakfast and lunch, and lunch and dinner. Today Panera operates the largest free wireless network in the United States. Subsequently Panera Bread Co. has become a "Coffice" for many. Yep, that's what some call it, when you go to a coffee shop and use it as your primary internet connection for business purposes, it's called a coffice, or that's was I was told. In the natural progression of technology, Wi-Fi is becoming a norm everywhere and added with the evolution of cloud computing it makes it possible to run ones coffice from a Panera café. I am certainly not advocating moving your office to the nearest Bread Co., but I always enjoy heading to Panera to pair a cup of coffee with a fresh pastry and enjoy free Wi-Fi access. Of course, Panera is not trying to become a coffice of any sort, but it has successfully executing the concept of a "third place", i.e., a location other than home and work where one can relax, meet and chat. While laptop and mobile users may appreciate the free internet access, offering Wi-Fi turns out to be more that an altruistic customer service gesture. Panera's timely combination of food and internet access may be the greatest thing since, well, sliced bread!

Today in a common person's world the mention of Wi-Fi immediately tones with Panera restaurant, instead of Cisco or even Airport. Now that's the power of Panera's branding and differential strategy. Free Wi-Fi is indeed an effective way to get customers in the door, but it brings along with it a host of problems. For any business customer service is the lifeblood and at Panera it's the attitude, so they had to be cautious as ambitious initiatives do have teething problems. Some folks might purchase nothing at all and stay for hours at a time, tying up tables that are especially needed during busy hours. In a customer service centric business, offering free Wi-Fi can be a tricky situation. That's why on the very first Wi-Fi connection page Panera requests its patrons to limit use during peak hours, and asks them to agree to the terms of use. In fact many locations restrict the duration of free Wi-Fi during peak hours to thirty minutes to an hour. Nonetheless, it's a point of pride for Panera to be able to continue to offer free Wi-Fi to all of their guests. Wi-Fi and the community gathering setup make Panera a great customer centric place. By the way, it costs the Bread Co. well over a million dollar annually for Internet expenses.

However, Panera's standing out on technology adaptation did not end with Wi-Fi. To help fulfill their business goals, Panera has incorporated numerous technology solutions over the years, changing its IT environment to meet evolving needs and as well taking advantage of technology advancements. Panera recognized early that technology, used properly, can help employees work more efficiently and ease customer frustrations. But the company didn't simply model its systems to focus on customer's transaction; there by it gave employees time for customer interaction. They use their in store enterprise application tool for labor scheduling and food cost management. It also provides corporate and retail operations management quick access to retail data, allows on-line ordering with distributors, and reduces managers' administrative time.

Then again, every Panera outlet has got the latest customer friendly point-of-sale registers, with product pricing being programmed from a remote location. These cool machines stockpiles tons of transaction data daily, which can be utilized to analyze pertinent information and business patterns. Panera's fresh dough facilities have matured information systems as well, which could seamlessly accept electronic orders and monitor delivery from their restaurant.

The Bread Co. is known for its many proprietary web based tools, such as eLearning, to provide on-line training for their associates and bakers. Additionally, they put into operation an impressive customer oriented Software-as-a-Service (SaaS) solution, which is essentially a combination of business and menu transaction analytics. Through that third party management system the management is able to quickly make key business decisions related to marketing, menu optimization, pricing, media buys, staffing and network planning. All these initiatives demonstrates that the company is motivated on providing customers with an outstanding experience, with the help of technology and innovation.

In terms of technology, Panera Bread Co. is well-rounded to say the least. Its technology solution implementation for security alarm system, which helps to reduce the incidence of break-ins is worth a mention. The interesting fact is, Panera's alarm systems are monitored at a remote site, utilizing Internet Protocol (IP), thereby preventing any potential coordinated physical attack at numerous store sites. The point is Panera plans way ahead in all aspects. Panera's operational excellence is the take away here.

Panera's IT leadership constantly evaluates its technology to ensure that employees and business are well equipped to serve customers. Behind the scenes, the focus on customers is just as apparent; the company has built its IT architecture to avoid downtime in branches, designed its applications to ensure seamless processing and apparently to enhance employee's interactions with customers and not to forget its cool smart phone application, the Nutrition Calculator.

Panera Bread® Nutrition Calculator is a brilliantly thought out initiative, which essentially amplifies Panera's customer first approach. If you love Panera Bread this fun and useful internet and smart phone application is a blessing. It calculates the nutritional value of any Panera meal quickly and easily, so as to make the best eating choice. In effect, it's empowering the customer using innovative technology. They know how to make you feel good about eating there; even after tossing down a 1000 calories Sierra Turkey sandwich! Panera has willingly shared full nutrition information on its website, even before any government requirement or regulations. Technology breakthroughs, particularly in the area of knowledge management, offer new and innovative ways to nurture customer relationships and Panera Bread® Nutrition Calculator is a great example.

Widespread use of the Internet has changed how customers expect relationship-building to work. Subsequently social media is radically changing the customer experience and interactions with companies at an accelerated speed. It's a serious business. Studies, by several independent business groups, support this claim. To a greater extent, consumers want support and product information via social media channels. More often than not, customers seen to trust company information provided to them in this manner. Estimates show that consumers are spending over a half of their online time on social networks and blogs. Sensing these trends, Panera quickly adjusted the way they communicate with their customers, and also ensured a delightful customer experience across these newly founded channels. Panera's in-house marketing team quickly understood that it was time to blend technology and social interaction for the co-creation of value. While social networking can seem overwhelming and hard to control, it provided a unique opportunity for its business, to deliver excellent customer service, in a cost effective way. By swiftly adopting social media strategies and providing customers with multiple trendy channels to interact, Panera Bead Co. successfully fostered customer loyalty on online community and adapting its business culture in the Web 2.0 world. Initially the online sweepstake tryout held just for its Facebook fans, which had more than 25,000 entries, shows Panera's creative social media adventure. It's worth to mention that Panera does "geo-target" messaging, which means a Chicago promotional message, for example, will only be sent to those who live in that city. When used precisely, such modern tools enable the company to individualize customer interactions in what's often referred to as "mass customization".

What's more, a new section on the company's webpage called "Stories and Tips", contributed by Panera's head baker, proves that their social media initiative is evolving into more than a marketing culture. Not to forget Panera Bread's YouTube channel, which features a variety of entertaining and informative videos. In fact Panera has established itself as a social media authority via social media marketing, thereby becoming an influencer in its business area. Panera's purposeful and carefully designed social media strategy has now become an integral part of its brand and marketing plan. I guess they found out that consumer loyalty is additionally strengthened when a company makes an online connection with their customers. Of course, more and more breakthrough technologies will be evolving in the future and at Panera they ensure that everything is only applied for embracing strong loyalty principles. Classic example is their trend-setting move on changing the way customers order fast food. Basically, Panera is combining store kiosks, online and mobile ordering so as to cut the number of cash registers. Though fast-food giants are also got similar plans of electronic ordering, Panera is aggressively ambitious in combining technologies which, is geared for speeding-up service. They call is Panera 2.0. The most visible change I noticed was the ordering kiosks being phased in at many Panera stores already. So obviously, there will be fewer cashiers in restaurants. So be prepared for the new experience as food orders will be delivered directly to tables, which isn't customary. And you guessed it right, former cashiers will now carry food to customer's tables. It's estimated that these tech upgrades costs about $125,000 per store. As always, Panera is on the cutting edge with the system. Mobile technology is the answer to boost customer service and reverse declining from a service bottleneck perspective. So I would say that the spending of over $42 million in technology upgrades to let customers order online or with their mobile devices and iPads is a timely winning move. It not only boosted general sales but encourages repeat customer visits and importantly discourages would-be diners from leaving before ordering (which happens a lot, as have seen a few time guests walking out because employees were too busy to take their orders). Nobody is going to go to a restaurant just because it has a cool mobile app. Technology in itself means nothing if it doesn't enable a differentiated customer experience. Panera was able to figure out how to use technology to enable a better guest experience and that's their winning game. Do you know that over fifty percent of their daily sales transactions occur on a Panera card? Which is golden data on individual purchase activities. Well then now the door is open for marketing and campaigns around individual consumers or small groups of consumers as opposed to the mass market. Under the pretext of automation and cost cutting, when many organizations are inadvertently isolating themselves from customer interactions, Panera Bread is opening more doors. Panera's passion in prudently exploiting technology, to deliver consistent customer experience, doesn't end with computers, internet and social media. The unique music that wafts through the bakery-cafes along with the aroma of fresh bread isn't synthesized or overly engineered. Their oasis environment, for the most part, is made up of acoustic guitar, real piano, some folk-forward, and songs you're familiar with, but probably won't hear on top radio stations or in elevators. Essentially they have every right to claim, "Panera bakery-cafe isn't just a place; it's a mood".

Chapter 5

Bread as a gift

"There is only one boss. The customer. And he can fire everybody in the company from the chairman on down, simply by spending his money somewhere else" - Sam Walton

The best things in life really are free! Take for instance, Panera's chicken, which are free of antibiotics. It is literally all natural, anti-biotic free chicken. While it can be a bit more expensive, there is certainly a difference in the taste (yes, it tastes like chicken). No wonder Panera is typically judged by some as a pricier chain. Anyway, to cover the increased cost and effort, Panera had to reluctantly hike sandwich prices by seven present or so. But Panera was able to raise prices as they cater to a higher-income customer base usually. Then again, anti-biotic free chicken did enhance the flavor profile of their menu. Naturally, it attracted more health conscious customers. Think about it, if you eat chicken that was raised on steroids then what are you putting in your body? Also, remember lard? It is indeed pig fat in a rendered form. So what would happen when french fries or chicken are fried in lard? One would take in some extra pork fat for free. Ok, let's not get too dramatic.

It's not fare to not to mention eggs here, i.e., more than seventy million eggs each year. After all "chicken or the egg dilemma" continues even in this Facebook age. At Panera, the eggs are also all-natural and cracked every morning. All hens that supply shell eggs and hard boiled eggs met the standard for "no antibiotics ever" and "vegetarian-only diet". I guess I need to stop here, as Panera's sausage is also all-natural (not their Applewood-smoked bacon though).

Then again to put things into perspective, approximately eight million pounds of "no antibiotics" pork and over two million pounds of "grass-fed" beef gets into Panara's supply chain annually.

Based on the company's pioneering "Food Policy", the Bread Co. regularly offers details regarding responsibly raised livestock and poultry. Which as well includes sharing progress planning on further reduction of antibiotic usage and confinement for farm animals in its supply chain for Panera Bread and St. Louis Bread Company bakery-cafes. It's worth mentioning here that Panera works closely with farmers and ranchers, to learn how to tangibly improve conditions for the procured farm animals. Thus intentionally reduced or eliminated the use of antibiotics and confinement.

As proudly mentioned on their Bakery-Cafe Menu, "With the skill of an artisan, the heat of the oven and a few fine ingredients, our bakers make bread that is simply delicious - and baked fresh every day", and that being the true state, one can never go wrong. No burger-and-fries or buckets of chicken to be seen on the menu, instead, soups, salads, and sandwiches and yet Panera Bread Co. is one hot restaurant today. Panera bakes more bread each day than any bakery-café concept in the country. On the other hand Panera recently improved its freshness of lettuce by cutting the time from field to plate in half. It is the same with the enhanced freshness of its breads by opting to fire up the ovens and bake all day. While Panera is hardly a new product mill, they had been constantly testing several new things. They had on the past surprised guests by way of Barbeque Chicken Chopped salad, Napa Almond Chicken Salad sandwich, Chipotle Chicken sandwich, Heart-of-the-Romaine lettuce, the low-cal Power Breakfast sandwich, Power Smoothie, Pecan Braid pastry, and so on. And if the rumor I heard turns out to be true, there could be a salmon sandwich soon. Who knows? We might even see zero-nitrate deli meats. Of course, Panera isn't the first to try all this, but it sure knows how to keep the food experience exciting. Panera's menu policy is a good example of an evolving origination based on customer's pulse. Thus Panera will always be ahead of the competition curve and that's the emphasis on this chapter, i.e. innovation.

Panera Bread Co. builds competitive advantage by restlessly strengthening its value, "the Panera way". Even during rather unfriendly economic season, Panera was consistent on offering guests its "total experience". It is because of that mindset there is always some kind of innovative expansion with their menu. Panera habitually chose to stay the course and continue to execute their long-term strategy of expanding their business, so as to benefit the customers.

For the company, bread is their platform and the entry point towards the Panera experience. Bread is the symbol of their quality and a reminder of Panera "Warmth", the totality of the experience the customer receives and can take home to share with friends and family. They strive to offer a memorable experience with superior customer service, there by to achieve unique "concept essence". It's rather their unpublished blueprint for attracting and retaining targeted customers that they believe appreciate Panera. Obviously, bread is their soul and expertise that makes all of their other food special.

Panera's competitive strengths are more than just great food at the right price. It is even more than their inviting and embracing culture. By which I mean, their dynamite menu innovation. It's value-oriented café, bakery and beverage menus are mostly designed to provide customers with rightly priced products built on the strength of their authentic bakery expertise. As a rule they feature a menu containing proprietary items prepared with high-quality, fresh ingredients, including my preferred anti-biotic free chicken, as well as unique recipes and toppings designed to provide appealing, flavorful products that would crave for more.
The important aspect is that they regularly review and update the menu offerings to satisfy changing customer preferences. They seek to continuously improve their products, or develop new ones, such as the recent heart-

of-the-romaine lettuce, reformulated French baguette, and the very latest Napa Almond Chicken Salad sandwich. Not to forget, new product rollouts are integrated into periodic or seasonal menu rotations. Like the already vanished Chopped Cobb Salad and Barbeque Chicken, Parisian Chicken soup, Fresh Strawberry Citrus pastry, Pumpkin Spice latte. Panera's menu innovation is one important reason that their value scores with customers remain so strong and unfailing.

Clearly, beyond bread, the focus on quality extends to the rest of Panera's menu. Panera was one of the first national concepts to remove trans fats from its entire menu. Quality bread products is the centerpiece of their menu, which also includes a wide variety of year-round favorites complemented by new items introduced seasonally. Panera seriously concentrates on internal innovation to continuously improve its menu, for an exceptional customer experience. Their menu lineup is always exciting with many of the new breads, sandwiches, soups and salads introduced regularly. At least five times per year there is a rotation of two specialty flavors. That's the result of internal innovation driven by customer's needs. Bread Co. thus continues to be a leader and trend-setter in the fast-casual segment. Then again, I should confess, Starbucks coffee is much better than Panera's. But then, there is a reason that Starbucks can't do baked goods and Panera.

Getting back on Panera's innovation model, the Via Panera catering business is perhaps the best example of Panera's boundless menu innovation. Their initial piloting of the flatbread pizza, called Crispani, was not an exactly a runway hit. Despite great fanfare, the product unfortunately tanked. Besides, even during the peak "Atkins diet" season Panera did what it could to keep health-conscious customers happy by developing low-carb items. Then again just like their bakery-cafes, a wide variety of breakfast and lunch options are offered. The difference lies however in the packaging and option for delivery. Interestingly the packaging includes paper goods (like plates, napkins and utensils) and a pleasant eye appealing layout, which makes planning easy and presentation phenomenal.

Not to forget their loyalty program, "MyPanera Customer Rewards", which essentially repays customers for eating at Panera. Well, not exactly, but as one would have guessed, the more a customer visits a location, the more complimentary bakery or café items, exclusive previews and tastings or cooking and baking tips they would receive. But what one would not guess is the integrated fun element, as there is a surprise when a reward has been earned. Panera associates would inform patrons when they place their order if they have a reward loaded onto their card. Actually more; guess who gets to preview their new commercials? It's the roughly estimated fifteen million customers, who belong to the MyPanera program.

The line of reasoning is, the customer centric menu along with Panera's efficient operating systems, and real estate strategy allows them to compete successfully in all segments of the restaurant business, including take home, through both on-premise sales and Via Panera catering. They essentially compete with specialty food, casual dining, and quick-service restaurant retailers, including national, regional and locally-owned restaurants. Panera's goal is always to be the best competitive alternative for customers craving soup, salad, or sandwiches. But as I started studying more about Panera's business experience, what hit me first was the missing mirror image. Yes, Panera doesn't have a real comparable rival; no direct national competitor that does what Panera Bread Co. does. It isn't a surprise why leading food reviewers and polling organizations such as Zagat, Harris Poll, J.D. Powers, Sandelman & Associates, BusinessWeek and QSR recognizes Panera every year.

So why doesn't one of the most successful restaurant chains have a direct hands-on competitor? Well, it's "the Panera way", which seems simple but is actually tough and hard to replicate its essence, i.e., a place to gather. On an average day they serve over twelve million people. Quality and consistently plays a huge role. And it's about striving to make food better with an innovative culture and impulse add-on initiatives. Panera is always focused on differentiation through innovative menu, utilizing new procedures to further improve produce quality. Thus keeps up and in most occasions exceeds customer expectations. Panera indeed serves up a 360-degree customer experience and it's a business lesson to be observed. However, Panera like any other business establishment is not immune from competition. In fact a big bulls-eye has been placed on its back, and that shouldn't surprise anyone, in any case not Panera Bread Co themselves. They indeed have got to compete with traditional fast food chains, as well as specialty food cafes, casual dine in restaurants, street vendors, pizza parlors, bakeries, and national, regional and locally-owned restaurants. Actually, many of the company's competitors have greater financial resources, which translate into greater advertising capacity.

Panera not only builds relationships but also delivers advice of healthy eating, via its products. When I mention product, I do mean Panera's great food, at a reasonable price, in a short amount of time. Everyone would agree, that there's something about having a sandwich on fresh baked bread that makes the difference. There are over a twenty fresh-dough manufacturing facilities located across the country that supplies bread and bakery goods to each store everyday. Panera could very well decide to turn around and do frozen dough, or just bake two to three times a week as opposed to everyday, which would be a great cost savings for the company. But that's the clever part, as Panera would not let that happen, as it would be quickly felt on the customer end. Actually the wave of "Paneranoia" is a game changer. These days one could taste its foot pint in the ciabatta roll of Wendy's Frescata sandwich and the Dijon horseradish sauce of Subway's Selects line. It's in the Premium salads at McDonald's and iced BK Joe at Burger King, the panini at Sheetz's convenience restaurant and the wraps at Wawa's stores. Panera's customer centric menu effect clearly had a slow but serious counter-response. The burger guys have all responded. If you would have noticed, oddly everyone has started to follow Panera style by broadening their menu with offerings that are certainly trying to be a higher-quality, premium product: premium sandwiches, premium salads, and now they're rolling out premium coffees as well.

No doubt, Panera attracts its crowds by focusing on freshness. Certainly attributes like consistent taste of food, cleanliness of restaurant and order accuracy helps the invocative menu lineup. But Panera's customer-centric product is further complimented with the kickoff concept of "Third Place". Warm-toned walls, soft lighting, natural wood tones and a fireplace, the decorative hallmarks of Panera Bread's bakery-cafes seem ubiquitous now, but that doesn't disguise the concept's essential genius. The design of Panera outlets displays their driving attributes, i.e., warm, authentic, comfortable and home. I think they've done a great job in spicing up our modern life style by creating that so-called third place.

On that note, if you redirect your attention from all the tempting breads and pastries for a moment to the walls of Panera dining room, a sampling from their personal collection of bread-based art can be appreciated. Perhaps it could be the world's foremost gallery of bread-based art. The original is usually displayed at Panera's support center in St. Louis, and reproductions are used in appropriate bakery-cafe locations (now, that's a cool insider information). All of their pieces, which range from paintings in various styles to photographs, sculpture, and mixed media, has bread as its central theme. But the interesting element is that much of it comes from up-and-coming local artists. Whenever possible, they look to the community surrounding their respective stores to find them. Now, isn't that just awesome?

The product offering and the level of innovation by the Bread Co. is indeed fit for a great business study. Despite all these successes Panera leadership doesn't believe that their "product" has hit its potential, and that's the beauty of true success.

Panera Bread is without a doubt the new trend in the restaurant industry, with fresh ingredients and quality food at prices similar or slightly above the average burger joint. No wonder they are growing faster than traditional fast-food restaurants. Panera's concept essentially hit on all cylinders. Not to forget their growing drive-through, in effect to better serve busy moms. People in communities across the U.S. now look to Panera Bread Co. as their neighborhood bakery-café. They are embracing Panera and its inviting, neighborly atmosphere, coming to the restaurant to spend a quiet moment, to meet friends over coffee, or to share a meal with family members. There was a time when there were many neighborhood ethnic bakeries and for the most part, they all slowly vanished. And then came giant supermarkets, which of course had bakery products, but it was never quite the same, until Panera came in. In my estimate, Panera is no way near its potential peak and it leaves me to wonder why Panera hasn't crossed overseas (of course not counting Canada). I also wonder, why there is no "scaled-back" version of Bread Co. at the airports!

Chapter 6

One Loaf at a Time

"Bread is the king of the table and all else is merely the court that surrounds the king. The countries are the soup, the meat, the vegetables, the salad but bread is king" - Louis Bromfield, (1896-1956)

The famous American novelist and painter, Henry Valentine Miller, few decades ago said, "You can travel fifty thousand miles in America without once tasting a piece of good bread". But, take heart, that's not the case any more and maybe Mr. Miller wouldn't get frustrated, for lack of good bread, if he had lived today. Thanks to Panera Bread Company and their customer focused culture.

So what did we gather thus far from the Panera experience?

To put everything in perspective, the attributes for consistent high customer approval ratings earned by Panera Bread Company are employee satisfaction, corporate citizenship, technology and product innovation; of course with a dash of proactive efforts on each.

No single factor led them to success. However, their timely customer oriented thinking combined with strong business leadership created a synergy that multiplied the impact. Most people probably think they know what Panera Bread Company does. However, Panera has quite a different idea of what its business is all about. In their view, the business it is involved in is customer satisfaction. Many business pundits were won over by the belief that terms like customer loyalty and customer experience has forever vanished and that the lowest price is the only thing that keeps a customer returning. But Panera proved them all wrong by demonstrating a neat customer focused business. And yes, customer loyalty is alive and well. Sure, in today's social media marketplace, creating and maintaining status quo ante is more complex than ever. Thus customer satisfaction alone is not necessarily enough for a sustainable business success.

At Panera Bread Company, customer service is a proactive model and so they are able to catch-up with modern empowered customers with ease. The company not only believed in the true principles of building long term customer relationship but, also whenever required, took a balanced approach with perceived panacea or silver bullet. My observation is that Panera consciously doesn't attempt any kind of quick fix in the area of customer service or brand marketing. Part of the credit goes to the company's leadership thinking as even during hard times they don't panic or display confusion, or an urgent search for perceived better ways. That could be the reasoning for their proactive customer centric approach.

Panera leadership, though to great extent, assumes that a positive correlation exists between customer satisfaction and customer behavior, also understand that such a correlation is not 100% reliable. They clearly understand customer retention and total share of customer are essential for repeat customers and so pursuing for market share isn't a priority. And that's exactly the mindset why the company is able to unswervingly find a strong relationship between its customer satisfaction measures and economic performance. They also make sure not to showcase their product as a commodity thereby bonding with their brand-loyal customers enduringly. Panera Bread business was carefully designed to appeal to all senses of an average repeat customer. The company doesn't think of bread as a product that was bagged and sent home with the groceries, and that can be sensed immediately after entering Panera Bread. They believe in real value and thus able to retain loyal customers. Panera is very calculative by not creating an atmosphere where their customers hunt for lowest price eating place. They are very well aware customers who respond only to price cutting may stir up orders, but they seldom become loyal customers. Panera as a brand constantly emphasizes the value of its products, thus displaying that it is interested in building a relationship with its customers. The customers are always kept at the top of all strategic planning and they strive to offer a memorable experience with proactive customer service approach.

Proactive customer care makes a huge difference to a customer's perception of the business establishment. At Panera its front line staff are trained and motivated to understand the significance of a proactive approach when dealing with customers. Of course, reactive customer service and problem-solving abilities are great and have their place in the scheme of customer experience, which am not discounting. But think about it, proactive service initiative could prevent that very same issue from arising. In any case, a pre-emptive act normally leads to significant savings of time and effort. At Panera, with an established proactive customer service mechanism, they noticed an increase in the efficiency of customer-facing staff as inquiries and problems are pre-empted and routine activities are reduced. A proactive approach to customer service is a choice that Panera Bread Company made in order to try and retain customer loyalty. Like any other business organization, it took some time for their staff trained to be reactive in their response to get out of that mode. Yet, it was achieved and proved to be a great way to maximize customer relationships. Panera employee's preemptive customer service can be felt the very second one enters their restaurant. Today Panera one amount the best-in-class customer service organizations which as customer experience to a new level.

Panera Bread® Nutrition Calculator is a classic example of proactive customer focused approach, utilizing internet technology. Panera Bread Foundation's Panera Cares is a unique endeavor where corporative citizenship is taken to the next level. Introduction of antibiotic-free chicken, which is sold in most Company-owned and franchise-operated bakery-cafes, is yet another example of proactive customer initiative based on product innovation. Though such chicken is more expensive and given that every business expert predicting Panera's chicken was doomed to fail, things proved the other way. It turns out Panera's consumers understand the value of paying more. That's why I strongly believe, Panera is always ahead of the curve understanding customer's pulse. The emergence of the Internet as a channel for customer service and timely utilization by Panera also gave new opportunities for improving the service efficiency. The basic fact that customers enjoy Panera's warm and welcoming environment featuring comfortable gathering areas, relaxing decor, and free internet access provided through a managed Wi-Fi network is itself the height of proactive thinking.

There's the old anecdote about two hikers and a bear. Two hikers in a backcountry trail, stop to rest. Hearing a rustling in the bushes, they crane for a better view and see two bear cubs playing near a stream. One of the men wheels around, freezes in terror and jabs his buddy in the ribs. It's the mama grizzly bear! Before either man has time to react, the mama charges towards them. One totally terrified guy stands motionless and panic-stricken. The other companion quickly tears off his hiking boots, digs into his backpack, pulls out a pair of tennis shoes, and quickly laces them up. His buddy is stunned. "There's no way you're going to outrun that mama grizzly!" he cries. "I don't have to outrun her," his companion responds. "I only have to outrun you!" The moral of the story is clear, think and stay ahead, and let circumstances beyond your control affect the unprepared.

Restaurant industry is one of the toughest businesses out there. Epically during hard-hitting economy, the untold strategy for most regional restaurant chains is to "just survive." As we've seen in any bad economy, the industry norm has always been cutting costs and, in many cases, closing stores. But Panera settled for an opposite line of attack. That is why, even during uncontrollable circumstances they take care of their customer and to make sure its loyal fan club is healthy. At Panera when mistakes are made, it's acknowledged and faced head on immediately. To ignore or deny that a problem has occurred without a doubt is damaging. Customers will abandon the business and brand. But the worst is, they will share their story with the world and that could become a full fledged public relations fiasco on tackle.

Panera typically handles customer complaints with style, but its leadership recognizes that waiting to hear from customers reactively does not give a realistic view of their operations. Like for every vocal customer that complains, there is a hidden army of silent customers who potentially could walk away and take their business elsewhere. Panera's goal of proactive support is to identify and resolve issues before they become problems.

In many instances, what I grasped was, they solved problems before customers even realize they exist. Of course, it is more labor intensive to provide this type of proactive service, and it means doing more than just what others do. But it earns the opportunity to stop the spread of negative word-of-mouth. Panera's proactive customer-centric thinking integrated with its product and work culture increased brand recognition, and certainly, business opportunities. It is so integrated that its employees seem to have a natural ability to head off problems before they happen. This proactive approach actually allows Panera to support more customers within existing staffing levels compared to its competitors.

Proactive customer service has always been a good strategy for Panera Bread Company. Then again it's only commonsense that reacting to problems after they occur is usually more expensive than addressing them proactively. It also usually means that the problem gets bigger than it would have been if it got nipped in the bud. That's the principle Panera applies to its customer service attitude.

Very early in the business Panera Bread Company appreciated the idea of becoming truly proactive. They had a clear vision of what Proactive Customer Service is and how it can be achieved. They also had strong management level champions who can lead the transition to proactive service and ensure that the objectives of that transition are actually achieved. Panera always had the habit of educating staff about customer service techniques and processes as they always knew how valuable customer loyalty is. Thus they consistently responded positively to growing pressures and emerging opportunities. Proactive customer service clearly offers a powerful strategy for exceeding customer expectations, reducing costs and supporting profitable business growth. In addition, several business studies find that higher customer satisfaction has a direct impact on employee motivation and loyalty. It's a cyclic effect on many levels.

Panera (before purchased by Au Bon Pain Co.) literally began with an effortless creative dream of one man. That dream was strongly cherished and nurtured, and today the dream itself grew into something beyond anybody's imagination. Panera Bread Company is built of an exciting vision, "warmth", which is about serving others. Even as the company got bigger quickly, they didn't swing over from their original vision of serving their customers. Subsequently, they matured into a unique customer culture, based on core values and commonsense beliefs, which have been embedded into the very fabric of Panera. The company demonstrates a genuine commitment to its employees as well. Every one at every level is treated with respect and dignity. Panera underscore and reinforces with all associates that they much have a desire to satisfy every single customer every day, no matter what. There is a passion for excellence and that can be seen in Panera's innovative menu lineups. They are always striving to do better on the customer service front and as a result they embrace healthy business changes or processes proactively. They have a can-do attitude on every aspect their business. And that is driven by even top officers being appropriately involved in the frontline details. Panera also invested fittingly in the practical application of technology, which is technology focused on customer experience.

Panera's success is clear, with combination of attributes like leading with values, strategic focus, leadership excellence, professional growth for employees, brand cultivation, and corporate citizenship duties. The company's quest for excellence combined by their natural acts of excellent customer service ended up not just revolutionizing the restaurant industry but the way-of-life for millions of its customers.

The ongoing success of Panera Bread Company literally means that there is little need for change. Now tell me for how many organizations can be associated with kind of a statement? It doesn't matter what the business is, it is essential that the primary motivation and leadership should be based on the positive impact it will earn for the customer. The customer is the only reason for anyone to even think about starting a business. To succeed, and then to sustain the success attained, it is vital that everyone on the team be passionate about the customer. So, if a customer is wrong, let them be wrong with dignity.

So as we close this book, let me mention a cool Panera story. The Bread Co's CEO, Ron Shaich, couple of years embarked on a quest to spend a week living on food stamps (well i.e. to live on just $4.50 a day). Actually it was for the SNAP Challenge, for the "Hunger Action Month" organized by the Supplemental Nutrition Assistance Program (formerly known as Food Stamps). The challenge has now become a popular way to see how the many less privileged folks essentially live and call attention to hunger issues. For Panera it's not new when it comes to tackle issues of food insecurity in the past; notably its "pay what you want" program at some of its locations. Anyway, as Shaich had the view of how the poorest of the poor live, my point is he wasn't able to have lunch at Panera all that week (with budget $31.50).

www.ingramcontent.com/pod-product-compliance
Lightning Source LLC
Chambersburg PA
CBHW022003170526
45157CB00003B/1124